EMMANUEL JOSEPH

The Creative Compass, Making Bold Decisions, Practicing Self-Compassion, and Building Stronger Communities.

Copyright © 2025 by Emmanuel Joseph

All rights reserved. No part of this publication may be reproduced, stored or transmitted in any form or by any means, electronic, mechanical, photocopying, recording, scanning, or otherwise without written permission from the publisher. It is illegal to copy this book, post it to a website, or distribute it by any other means without permission.

First edition

*This book was professionally typeset on Reedsy.
Find out more at reedsy.com*

Contents

1	Chapter 1: Embracing Creativity	1
2	Chapter 2: The Power of Bold Decisions	3
3	Chapter 3: Self-Compassion: The Key to Resilience	5
4	Chapter 4: Building Stronger Communities Through Creative...	7
5	Chapter 5: Overcoming Creative Blocks	9
6	Chapter 6: The Intersection of Creativity and Leadership	10
7	Chapter 7: Cultivating a Creative Environment	12
8	Chapter 8: The Role of Mindfulness in Creativity	14
9	Chapter 9: Balancing Creativity and Practicality	16
10	Chapter 10: The Impact of Creativity on Personal Growth	18
11	Chapter 11: Creative Problem-Solving Techniques	19
12	Chapter 12: The Connection Between Creativity and Emotional...	21
13	Chapter 13: Inspiring Creativity in Others	22
14	Chapter 14: The Benefits of Creative Pursuits for Mental...	23
15	Chapter 15: The Role of Creativity in Social Change	24
16	Chapter 16: Celebrating Creative Achievements	26
17	Chapter 17: The Future of Creativity and Bold...	28

1

Chapter 1: Embracing Creativity

Creativity is the cornerstone of human progress. It enables us to envision new possibilities and explore uncharted territories. Understanding that everyone has a unique creative potential is the first step toward making bold decisions. By nurturing our creative instincts, we can transform our lives and our communities.

In today's fast-paced world, the ability to think creatively has never been more important. Creativity is not confined to the arts; it permeates every aspect of our lives, from problem-solving at work to finding innovative ways to connect with others. To embrace creativity, we must first recognize its value and cultivate an open mind.

One effective way to nurture creativity is to engage in activities that stimulate the mind. This could be anything from reading diverse genres of literature to exploring different cultures and perspectives. By exposing ourselves to new ideas and experiences, we can broaden our horizons and fuel our creative thinking.

Another crucial aspect of embracing creativity is to allow ourselves the freedom to experiment and make mistakes. Fear of failure can stifle creativity, but by adopting a growth mindset, we can view challenges as opportunities for learning and growth. Encouraging a culture of experimentation, both personally and within our communities, can lead to innovative solutions and breakthroughs.

THE CREATIVE COMPASS, MAKING BOLD DECISIONS, PRACTICING SELF-COMPASSION, AND BUILDING STRONGER COMMUNITIES.

By understanding and nurturing our creative potential, we can make bold decisions that drive personal and communal growth. Embracing creativity is not just about coming up with new ideas; it is about having the courage to pursue them and the resilience to overcome obstacles along the way.

2

Chapter 2: The Power of Bold Decisions

Making bold decisions often involves stepping out of our comfort zones. The psychology behind decision-making reveals that humans are naturally inclined to avoid risk. However, taking risks is essential for growth and progress. This chapter delves into the importance of making bold decisions and how they can lead to significant personal and community growth.

Bold decisions require a certain level of courage and confidence. This confidence often stems from a strong belief in our abilities and the value of our ideas. By cultivating self-awareness and understanding our strengths, we can make more informed and confident decisions. Moreover, seeking support from mentors and peers can provide valuable perspectives and encouragement.

The stories of individuals who have made courageous choices serve as powerful inspiration. From entrepreneurs who have started successful businesses to activists who have driven social change, these examples highlight the transformative power of bold decisions. These individuals demonstrate that while the path may be challenging, the rewards can be immense.

Overcoming fear and doubt is a crucial part of making bold decisions. Techniques such as mindfulness and visualization can help manage anxiety and build mental resilience. By focusing on our long-term goals and values, we can stay motivated and committed to our decisions, even in the face of adversity.

3

Chapter 3: Self-Compassion: The Key to Resilience

Self-compassion is a vital component of emotional well-being. It allows us to treat ourselves with kindness and understanding, especially during challenging times. This chapter discusses the benefits of self-compassion and how it can enhance our ability to make bold decisions.

Self-compassion involves recognizing our own suffering and responding with care and empathy. It means acknowledging our mistakes and imperfections without harsh judgment. By cultivating self-compassion, we can build resilience and cope with life's ups and downs more effectively.

One way to practice self-compassion is through self-reflection. Taking the time to understand our emotions and experiences can help us develop a more compassionate mindset. This can be done through journaling, meditation, or simply taking a moment to pause and breathe.

Another important aspect of self-compassion is self-care. Prioritizing our physical, emotional, and mental well-being can help us feel more balanced and grounded. This can include activities such as exercise, hobbies, or spending time with loved ones. By taking care of ourselves, we can better support others and make more thoughtful decisions.

Building a self-compassionate mindset takes time and practice, but the rewards are immense. By treating ourselves with kindness and understanding, we can cultivate resilience, make bold decisions, and build stronger communities.

4

Chapter 4: Building Stronger Communities Through Creative Collaboration

Communities thrive when individuals come together to share their talents and ideas. This chapter explores the role of creativity in fostering collaboration and building stronger, more resilient communities.

Creative collaboration involves working together to solve problems, generate new ideas, and create meaningful change. It requires open communication, trust, and a willingness to listen and learn from others. By fostering a collaborative mindset, communities can achieve greater innovation and progress.

One way to encourage creative collaboration is to create opportunities for people to connect and share their ideas. This can be done through community events, workshops, or online platforms. By providing spaces for collaboration, individuals can come together to brainstorm, experiment, and develop new solutions.

Inclusivity and diversity are also crucial for successful collaboration. By embracing different perspectives and experiences, communities can benefit from a wider range of ideas and insights. This can lead to more innovative and effective solutions to challenges.

Creative collaboration not only strengthens communities but also empowers individuals to contribute their unique talents and skills. By working together, we can build stronger, more resilient communities that thrive on creativity and innovation.

5

Chapter 5: Overcoming Creative Blocks

Creative blocks can hinder our ability to innovate and make bold decisions. This chapter identifies common causes of creative blocks and offers practical solutions to overcome them.

Creative blocks often stem from fear of failure, self-doubt, or external pressures. Recognizing these obstacles is the first step toward overcoming them. By understanding the root causes of creative blocks, we can develop strategies to address them.

One effective way to overcome creative blocks is to change our environment. A new setting can provide fresh inspiration and help us see things from a different perspective. This can be as simple as taking a walk, rearranging our workspace, or seeking out new experiences.

Another strategy is to practice mindfulness and relaxation techniques. Stress and anxiety can inhibit creativity, so finding ways to relax and clear our minds can help us tap into our creative potential. Techniques such as meditation, deep breathing, or even taking breaks can be beneficial.

Maintaining a growth mindset is also crucial for overcoming creative blocks. Viewing challenges as opportunities for learning and growth can help us stay motivated and open to new ideas. By adopting a positive and resilient attitude, we can navigate creative blocks and unlock our full creative potential.

6

Chapter 6: The Intersection of Creativity and Leadership

Effective leaders harness the power of creativity to inspire and guide their teams. This chapter examines the relationship between creativity and leadership, highlighting the qualities of creative leaders.

Creative leaders possess a unique blend of vision, empathy, and adaptability. They are able to see beyond the status quo and envision new possibilities. By fostering a culture of creativity, these leaders can inspire their teams to think innovatively and collaborate effectively.

One key quality of creative leaders is the ability to listen and understand the needs and perspectives of their team members. By creating an inclusive and supportive environment, they can encourage open communication and diverse thinking. This leads to more innovative solutions and a stronger sense of team cohesion.

Another important aspect of creative leadership is the willingness to take risks and embrace change. Creative leaders are not afraid to challenge conventional thinking and explore new ideas. By being open to experimentation and learning from failures, they can drive continuous improvement and growth.

Creative leadership is not just about having innovative ideas; it is about empowering others to reach their full potential. By fostering a culture

CHAPTER 6: THE INTERSECTION OF CREATIVITY AND LEADERSHIP

of creativity and collaboration, leaders can inspire their teams to achieve remarkable results and drive positive change.

7

Chapter 7: Cultivating a Creative Environment

A supportive environment is essential for nurturing creativity. This chapter explores ways to create spaces that encourage creative thinking and innovation. It discusses the impact of physical and social environments on creativity and provides practical advice for cultivating a creative atmosphere at home, work, and in the community.

The physical environment plays a significant role in fostering creativity. Designing spaces that are open, flexible, and filled with natural light can stimulate creative thinking. Adding elements such as plants, art, and comfortable seating can create a welcoming and inspiring atmosphere. By creating a space that feels inviting, we can encourage ourselves and others to engage in creative activities.

Social environments are equally important in nurturing creativity. Surrounding ourselves with supportive and like-minded individuals can inspire us to think creatively and take risks. Building a network of creative peers and mentors can provide valuable feedback, encouragement, and collaboration opportunities. By fostering positive relationships and a sense of community, we can create a fertile ground for creative ideas to flourish.

Creating a culture of curiosity and experimentation is also crucial for cultivating a creative environment. Encouraging exploration, questioning,

CHAPTER 7: CULTIVATING A CREATIVE ENVIRONMENT

and trying new things can lead to innovative solutions and discoveries. By celebrating creativity and recognizing its value, we can inspire others to embrace their own creative potential.

8

Chapter 8: The Role of Mindfulness in Creativity

Mindfulness practices can enhance our creative abilities by helping us stay present and focused. This chapter delves into the connection between mindfulness and creativity, offering techniques for incorporating mindfulness into daily routines.

Mindfulness involves paying attention to the present moment without judgment. By practicing mindfulness, we can develop greater awareness of our thoughts, emotions, and surroundings. This heightened awareness can lead to deeper insights and more original ideas.

One way to incorporate mindfulness into our daily routines is through meditation. Setting aside a few minutes each day to meditate can help us clear our minds and reduce stress. This mental clarity can enhance our ability to think creatively and solve problems.

Another technique is to practice mindfulness during everyday activities. Whether it's walking, eating, or working, we can bring a mindful attitude to these tasks by focusing on the present moment and fully engaging with our experiences. This can help us stay open to new ideas and inspirations.

Mindfulness can also improve our ability to manage distractions and stay focused on our creative projects. By developing greater concentration and mental resilience, we can enhance our creative potential and achieve more

CHAPTER 8: THE ROLE OF MINDFULNESS IN CREATIVITY

meaningful results.

9

Chapter 9: Balancing Creativity and Practicality

While creativity is essential for innovation, it must be balanced with practicality to achieve tangible results. This chapter discusses the importance of integrating creative ideas with realistic plans and goals.

Balancing creativity and practicality involves finding the right harmony between imaginative thinking and practical execution. This requires setting clear goals and developing actionable plans to achieve them. By breaking down creative ideas into manageable steps, we can ensure that our projects are both inspiring and achievable.

One strategy for balancing creativity and practicality is to use frameworks such as SMART goals (Specific, Measurable, Achievable, Relevant, and Time-bound). This approach helps us set clear objectives and track our progress, ensuring that our creative endeavors remain focused and on track.

Another important aspect is to seek feedback and refine our ideas. By sharing our creative concepts with others and being open to constructive criticism, we can identify potential challenges and make necessary adjustments. This iterative process can help us improve our ideas and increase their practicality.

Balancing creativity and practicality also involves managing our time and

CHAPTER 9: BALANCING CREATIVITY AND PRACTICALITY

resources effectively. Prioritizing tasks and setting realistic deadlines can help us stay organized and maintain momentum. By finding the right balance, we can turn our creative visions into reality.

10

Chapter 10: The Impact of Creativity on Personal Growth

Creativity is a powerful tool for personal development. This chapter explores how engaging in creative activities can lead to increased self-awareness, confidence, and fulfillment.

Engaging in creative pursuits allows us to express our thoughts, emotions, and ideas in unique ways. This self-expression can lead to greater self-awareness and understanding of our inner selves. By exploring different forms of creativity, such as writing, painting, or music, we can discover new aspects of our identity and expand our horizons.

Creativity also boosts our confidence by providing opportunities for accomplishment and recognition. Completing a creative project or receiving positive feedback can give us a sense of pride and achievement. This increased confidence can translate to other areas of our lives, enabling us to take on new challenges with a positive attitude.

In addition to self-awareness and confidence, creativity can bring a sense of fulfillment and joy. The process of creating something original and meaningful can be deeply satisfying and enriching. By making time for creative activities, we can enhance our overall well-being and lead more fulfilling lives.

11

Chapter 11: Creative Problem-Solving Techniques

Creative problem-solving is an essential skill for navigating complex challenges. This chapter introduces various techniques for approaching problems with a creative mindset.

One effective technique is brainstorming, which involves generating a wide range of ideas without immediate judgment or evaluation. This allows for free-flowing creativity and can lead to innovative solutions. Encouraging diverse perspectives during brainstorming sessions can also enhance the quality of ideas.

Mind mapping is another valuable tool for creative problem-solving. By visually organizing thoughts and ideas around a central concept, we can identify connections and patterns that may not be immediately apparent. This can help us see the bigger picture and explore different avenues for solving a problem.

Design thinking is a structured approach that combines empathy, creativity, and practicality. It involves understanding the needs of the end user, generating ideas, prototyping, and testing solutions. This iterative process allows for continuous improvement and refinement of ideas.

By incorporating these techniques into our problem-solving toolkit, we can approach challenges with a creative mindset and develop innovative solutions

THE CREATIVE COMPASS, MAKING BOLD DECISIONS, PRACTICING
SELF-COMPASSION, AND BUILDING STRONGER COMMUNITIES.

that address the root causes of issues.

12

Chapter 12: The Connection Between Creativity and Emotional Intelligence

Emotional intelligence plays a crucial role in our ability to harness creativity effectively. This chapter explores the relationship between creativity and emotional intelligence, highlighting the importance of self-awareness, empathy, and emotional regulation.

Self-awareness allows us to understand our emotions, strengths, and limitations. By being in tune with our inner selves, we can better navigate creative challenges and make more informed decisions. Practices such as journaling and meditation can help develop self-awareness.

Empathy, the ability to understand and share the feelings of others, enhances our creativity by broadening our perspective. By putting ourselves in others' shoes, we can generate ideas that resonate with diverse audiences and address their needs. Building strong relationships and actively listening to others can foster empathy.

Emotional regulation, the ability to manage and respond to our emotions, is essential for maintaining focus and resilience during the creative process. Techniques such as deep breathing, mindfulness, and positive self-talk can help us stay calm and centered, even in the face of setbacks.

By developing emotional intelligence, we can enhance our creative abilities and make more thoughtful and impactful decisions.

13

Chapter 13: Inspiring Creativity in Others

Inspiring creativity in others can lead to a more dynamic and innovative community. This chapter provides tips for encouraging and supporting the creative endeavors of those around us.

Creating a supportive environment is key to fostering creativity in others. This involves providing opportunities for individuals to express their ideas and collaborate on projects. Encouraging open communication and constructive feedback can help build confidence and trust.

Mentorship is another powerful way to inspire creativity. By sharing our knowledge and experiences, we can guide and motivate others to explore their creative potential. Offering support, encouragement, and resources can help mentees overcome challenges and achieve their goals.

Recognizing and celebrating creative achievements can also inspire further innovation. Acknowledging the efforts and successes of others can boost morale and motivation. This can be done through awards, public recognition, or simply expressing appreciation.

By nurturing and supporting the creativity of those around us, we can create a thriving and dynamic community that benefits from diverse ideas and perspectives.

14

Chapter 14: The Benefits of Creative Pursuits for Mental Health

Engaging in creative activities has been shown to have numerous mental health benefits. This chapter examines the positive impact of creativity on mental well-being, including reduced stress, increased happiness, and improved cognitive function.

Creative activities provide an outlet for self-expression and emotional release. Whether it's painting, writing, or playing music, engaging in these activities can help us process and cope with our emotions. This can lead to reduced stress and anxiety and an overall sense of well-being.

Creativity also promotes mindfulness and presence. When we fully immerse ourselves in a creative project, we can experience a state of flow, where we lose track of time and become completely absorbed in the task. This can lead to increased happiness and fulfillment.

Engaging in creative pursuits can also enhance cognitive function. Activities that challenge our brains, such as solving puzzles or learning a new skill, can improve memory, problem-solving abilities, and overall brain health.

By incorporating creative activities into our daily lives, we can enhance our mental well-being and lead more balanced and fulfilling lives.

15

Chapter 15: The Role of Creativity in Social Change

Creativity has the power to drive social change and address pressing societal issues. This chapter explores how creative approaches can be used to tackle challenges such as inequality, environmental sustainability, and community development.

Creative thinking allows us to envision new solutions to complex problems. By approaching societal issues with an open and innovative mindset, we can develop strategies that address the root causes of these challenges. This can lead to more effective and sustainable solutions.

One way creativity can drive social change is through art and storytelling. By raising awareness and inspiring action, creative expressions can bring attention to important issues and mobilize communities. Whether through visual art, music, or literature, creative works can challenge the status quo and inspire change.

Collaborative and inclusive approaches are also essential for creative social change. By involving diverse perspectives and engaging communities in the problem-solving process, we can develop solutions that are more equitable and effective. This can lead to greater social cohesion and resilience.

Creativity can also be harnessed to develop innovative technologies and practices that promote sustainability and social justice. By thinking outside

CHAPTER 15: THE ROLE OF CREATIVITY IN SOCIAL CHANGE

the box and challenging conventional approaches, we can create a more just and sustainable world.

16

Chapter 16: Celebrating Creative Achievements

Recognizing and celebrating creative achievements can inspire further innovation and growth. This chapter discusses the importance of acknowledging creative successes, both big and small.

Celebrating creativity involves recognizing the value and impact of creative endeavors. This can be done through awards, public recognition, or simply expressing appreciation. By acknowledging creative achievements, we can boost morale and motivation and inspire others to pursue their creative potential.

Sharing stories of creative success can also inspire and educate others. By highlighting examples of individuals and communities that have achieved remarkable results through creativity, we can provide role models and valuable insights. These stories can serve as a source of inspiration and encouragement for others to embark on their creative journeys.

Creating opportunities for showcasing creative work, such as exhibitions, performances, or publications, can also help celebrate and promote creativity. By providing platforms for creative expression, we can foster a culture of innovation and appreciation.

Recognizing and celebrating creative achievements is not just about the end results; it is also about valuing the process and effort involved. By appreciating

CHAPTER 16: CELEBRATING CREATIVE ACHIEVEMENTS

the dedication and perseverance required for creative endeavors, we can cultivate a supportive and encouraging environment for creativity to thrive.

17

Chapter 17: The Future of Creativity and Bold Decision-Making

As we look to the future, creativity and bold decision-making will continue to play a vital role in shaping our world. This chapter explores emerging trends and opportunities for creative innovation.

The rapid advancement of technology presents new opportunities for creative expression and problem-solving. From virtual reality and artificial intelligence to digital art and online collaboration, technology is expanding the possibilities for creativity. By embracing these innovations, we can explore new frontiers and develop groundbreaking solutions.

Global challenges such as climate change, social inequality, and economic instability require creative and bold approaches. By thinking creatively and making courageous decisions, we can develop strategies that address these pressing issues and create a more sustainable and equitable future.

Interdisciplinary collaboration will also be crucial for future creativity. By bringing together diverse fields and expertise, we can generate innovative ideas and solutions. This collaborative approach can lead to breakthroughs that transcend traditional boundaries and drive progress.

As we move forward, it is essential to foster a mindset of continuous learning and curiosity. By staying open to new ideas and embracing change, we can navigate uncertainty and seize opportunities for creative growth.

The future holds immense potential for creativity and bold decision-making. By harnessing our creative instincts and making courageous choices, we can build stronger communities and create a better world for future generations.

The Creative Compass: Making Bold Decisions, Practicing Self-Compassion, and Building Stronger Communities.

In a world that is ever-changing and filled with complexities, "The Creative Compass" is your guide to navigating life's challenges through creativity, bold decision-making, and self-compassion. This insightful book explores the power of creativity in shaping our personal and communal lives. It offers practical advice on how to cultivate your creative potential, make courageous choices, and foster a supportive and inclusive environment.

Through a blend of inspiring stories, practical strategies, and thought-provoking exercises, this book delves into the essential elements of creativity. It highlights the importance of self-compassion as a foundation for resilience and explores how creative collaboration can build stronger, more resilient communities. You'll discover techniques for overcoming creative blocks, balancing creativity with practicality, and using emotional intelligence to enhance your creative thinking.

"The Creative Compass" also examines the impact of creativity on personal growth, mental health, and social change. It provides valuable insights on how to inspire creativity in others and celebrate creative achievements. As you journey through the chapters, you'll gain the tools and confidence to embrace creativity in all aspects of your life and make bold decisions that drive positive change.

Whether you're an aspiring artist, a seasoned entrepreneur, or simply someone seeking to live a more creative and fulfilling life, "The Creative Compass" will empower you to unlock your full potential and contribute to a brighter, more innovative future.

www.ingramcontent.com/pod-product-compliance
Lightning Source LLC
LaVergne TN
LVHW020740090526
838202LV00057BA/6156